**How to Protect
Yourself with
KARATE**

How to Protect Yourself with
KARATE

by Craig Lomack

AN ESSANDESS SPECIAL EDITION
NEW YORK • 1967

CONTENTS

PART 3

Karate In Its Ultimate Use

How to Protect
Yourself with
KARATE

INTRODUCTION

THE RIGHT TO SURVIVE

"Terror In The Streets" is not just the discarded slogan of a fading political campaign. Every day the lives of thousands of citizens are forcibly involved in the tragic consequences of murder, rape, assault, and crippling injury.

Entire patterns of the life of this beautiful nation are being eroded by fear. Rarely can a man, at the finish of a day's work, ask his wife or child to stop by the local grocer's for a newspaper, cigarettes, or a six-pack. Instead of relaxing for the evening, he must go himself or make a special stop, before dinner, when he is hungry and tired. No more can the single woman or working mother leave the house after dark to purchase a late dinner or milk for the baby. In some areas, in fact, it is unsafe to go out in broad daylight.

Unfortunately, even seclusion is no longer a defense against this threat of terror. For our dwellings themselves have become vulnerable battlegrounds, and the locked door and window have ceased to be impediments to the criminal insanity of the bully-boy, the rapist, the child murderer, and the fiend. In homes and hallways, on country roads, in elevators, streets, and parks, the very plight of our people is at stake.

NO VOLUNTEER VICTIMS

Since the murder and sex attack, several years ago, of three middle-aged women, in a cave, by an otherwise apparently normal young man, one jarring observation has become increasingly evident: An expanding climate of physical terror is undermining the vital foundations of a secure and happy mode of American life.

Social scientists tell us that the sadist who stalks the woman and child is a sick man—although the question of why he should be permitted to communicate his perverted plague to the innocent has never been answered. But the most obvious thing about the rapist, sexual criminal, or child-assaulter is that he is a coward. He will not use his energies in the world of grown men, because *a man can fight back*. Since this type of criminal advances only into those areas of least resistance, it becomes urgent that every female in America prepare herself to offer swift, devastating resistance to this most disturbing category of crime.

She must begin preparation now, today, immediately, for by tomorrow morning the damage may have been done, and an avoidable personal disaster established as an irrevocable fact.

JOIN RANKS—REFUSE TO BE ABUSED

It is good common sense that the man who preys on the weak, on the defenseless woman and child, will cease and desist when the so-called weak begin to strike back. When the woman and child are no longer defenseless, the criminal coward will go back to exercising his evil on cats and birds.

Because of the fortunate discovery of Power Karate, you now have in your hands the potential ability to strike back—and to protect the life and person of yourself, your children, your loved ones.

The woman who ventures into today's lawless society without preparing herself to resist forcefully any attack is as negligent as a woman who would knowingly drive a car without brakes.

We have reached a time when it is vitally necessary that all of our citizens stand up among the ranks of civilized people confidently ready to resist, with firmness and vigor, the spreading anarchy of the criminal and sexual psychopath. In this way will the American woman spare herself the painful consequences and tragic aftermath of unlawful personal assault. In this way will each instance of successful resistance deter the coward and criminal and save many additional women and children from the same tragic circumstances.

UNCIVIL DEFENSE

The introduction of Power Karate is a milestone in the American woman's freedom of movement.

Power Karate makes the average woman capable of disabling an attacker with one or two explosive blows to his vulnerable areas. Her safety will not be dependent on the insane whim of a mugger-turned-rapist. Instead, she will be able to render an attacker helpless or crippled in a matter of seconds.

One cannot deal honestly with a thief or gently with a murderer. Power Karate places in a woman's hands that very power which enables her to deal with a potential killer on his own terms. The author does not believe in "fitting the punishment to the crime." Any man who would physically threaten a woman or child must be dealt with in the severest possible way. Otherwise what begins as a minor molestation may turn into a major attack. The practice of Power Karate for fifteen minutes a day, a few days a week, arms a woman with instant responses to contain any threat right on the spot.

FEMININE BUT NOT VULNERABLE

Through the ages men have been able to assert their physical will over women solely because of their superior size and strength —in the same way that very large men have been able to dominate men who are small.

Power Karate now gives women the right of self-defense, when in their judgment its use becomes necessary.

Because of Power Karate, size and strength have ceased to be critical factors in self-protection.

Power Karate was invented in eastern monasteries by monks whose religion denied them the use of arms. This was also a lawless time and it was impossible for these basically gentle men to leave their monasteries without being beset by armed bandits. These monks therefore developed the most devastatingly effective method of self-defense known to man. It has passed into our hands as Power Karate.

In the area of the world where Power Karate was discovered many of the people were of very small stature and slight bone structure. Thus, the system was not based on strength, but rather on a few rapid movements directed against an attacker's exposed areas. *The system of Power Karate, in fact, was built around the lack of extreme strength of the men who practiced it.* Many of the method's greatest experts, men who could defeat two or three armed opponents with quick, skillful movements of their empty hands, *actually weighed less than 110 pounds.* Thus, even a beginner's ability in the methods of Power Karate allows that a woman must never again be at the mercy of a criminal lunatic whose only advantage is superior strength. It has long been said that knowledge brings freedom, and the greatest freedom of all is the secure confidence that one's person is forever immune from outrageous attack.

ISOMETRIC POWER KARATE

Learning Power Karate, in your spare moments, in your own home, can prove a most pleasant experience. In the past, many women have shied away from self-defense programs. Even though women have recently become aware of the urgent need to possess some skill at self-protection, they have put off acquiring it because of a natural desire to remain feminine. Happily, this problem is now resolved. For in addition to its more serious objectives, Power Karate is also a perfect form of isometric exercise. The ancient monks who invented the system stumbled onto the principle of isometric exercise and incorporated it into the essence of karate practice.

In point of fact, because all Power Karate practice is *isometric* it acts as a perfect *balancer* for the woman. Isometric Power Karate will *shape up* arms, chest, and legs which may be on the lean side; it will equally *firm up* and reduce all contours in that group of women who have perhaps been a little indulgent in their choice of desserts. As has been observed before, with Power Karate there is a winner every time.

FRINGE BENEFITS

The return on your investment—in this case a little of your time and interest each week—is enormous. It is hard to put a value on the peace of mind that comes with confidence and, should the situation ever arise, the value of escaping unscathed from dire emergency is beyond measure. But like the iceberg which only reveals one-tenth of its bulk above the surface of the water, these returns are just the more obvious dividends accruing to the student of Power Karate.

Due to the isometric content of its movements, Power Karate reaches and stimulates literally scores of muscle groups that are ignored in other systems of exercise. By the same token the internal nature of the isometric karate movements reaches and stimulates the *internal* body. This includes such important health areas as the breathing and blood circulation processes, the heart and lungs and all essential organs, plus stimulation of vision, skin tone, and hair quality.

This easy, productive type of exercise is basic and essential to sound sleep, calm nerves, deep energy reserves, and healthfulness of appetite, digestion, and elimination. Whether your day is leisurely, or filled by employment, housework, and child care, you will find your karate workouts an invigorating and satisfying interlude in your daily routine.

Beyond fame and wealth, a secure mind in a sound, attractive, energetic body is the goal of everyone, man and woman alike. The pleasant practice of the movements of Power Karate places this goal within reaching distance of all. And, we might add, germinates that sparkling buoyancy of spirit which seems to be the secret quality that makes women, exclusive of physical appeal, so irresistible to men.

A REMINDER

Now that you have picked up this book, your life, in the realest possible sense, is in your hands.

Remember, karate saves lives.

PART 1

WOMEN'S EMERGENCY
KARATE SELF-DEFENSE

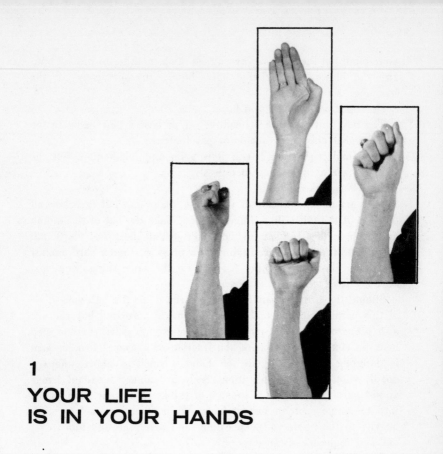

1
YOUR LIFE
IS IN YOUR HANDS

You are ironing. Outside it is just getting dark. You are alone. There are some noises near your door. No matter; if it's for you, they'll knock. The door is locked. Let's see; when you came back from the supermarket you put the two bags on the floor and locked the door behind you. Or did you first take the bags to the kitchen table and then go back and lock up? You were in the kitchen and had to start the potatoes.

The door opens.

A tall, dark, heavily built man walks through and is looking right at you. He says nothing but comes straight to you; you are too shocked to scream or even move. He reaches out and grabs your arm, pulling you to him. The feel of his hand triggers back your wits. You start to scream, but before any sound escapes a heavy hand clamps over your mouth and begins to bend you back. You begin to feel panicked and seek to break free, but nothing will prevail against that terrible strength. Half remembered advice flits through your mind but there is no way you can kick, nothing to bite or butt, and the blows of your free hand bounce meaninglessly off the stranger's shoulder.

He continues to bend you back. . . .

The next day you are a headline, or at best a new name in the appointment book of a doctor or psychiatrist.

Grim and frightening? Yes, it is grim and frightening. But the statistics are accumulating mercilessly.

However, make a fist.

Now extend the knuckle of your first finger one-half inch beyond the line of the other three fingers. Good. Take the flat of the thumb and place against the side of the finger so that the tip of the thumb and point of the finger are in line. Now press the thumb hard against the finger. Form your other fist and do the same thing. *You now have a killing weapon in either hand.*

Should the strange man, intent on harm, come through your door at this point, you turn to face him. You are surprised but you are also *prepared.* As he reaches out to seize your left arm you step back on your left leg. During the fraction of a second that his arm is dangling in the air your left hand, formed as above, snaps a deadly shot to his Adam's apple. As your stunned assailant hangs almost paralyzed, unable to breathe or think, your right hand zooms into the same spot an instant later. While your ex-assailant sinks heavily to the floor, you step calmly and *safely* around him to go out and request assistance.

Still vicious and grim? Certainly. But with one enormous difference. It is the attacker who is suffering the pain of his own chosen evil, while you and your loved ones have been spared the tragic aftermath of heedless abuse.

The secrets of Power Karate which enable a woman to mount a successful defense against a man twice her size are: mobility of power, concentration of power, and generation of power. These principles can be stated as follows:

1. Power Karate teaches how to form the hands into various weapons so that deadly blows can be struck repeatedly from any position, regardless of the position of the attacker. (The use of the legs will be dealt with in a later chapter.)

2. Power Karate teaches how to concentrate all of one's force, very briefly, and at one point of the body only—the striking surface—and how to bring this force to bear effectively on the attacker's weakest exposed area.

3. Power Karate reveals ancient and previously secret techniques of how to generate and focus striking force that makes the weakest person momentarily equal in hitting strength to the strongest person.

Note to keep in mind: Go for the soft spots: throat, eyes, groin, and solar plexus (center of body halfway between belt and tie clip).

You are the target of unprovoked attack; do not worry about protecting your attacker.

FORMING HANDS AS DEADLY WEAPONS

For success in an encounter, it is of the essence to be able to strike repeatedly into an opening. To do this without losing vital time in recovering and resetting arm position you must practice the various "hands" used in Power Karate. We will deal here with five.

Spear Hand:

Striking surface is tip of thumb and bony part of knuckle just below point. Keep wrist straight in practice but adjust angle to bear on striking point in actual use. Arm can be moved as unit from shoulder or snapped from elbow. Use against eyes, throat (Adam's apple), solar plexus, and especially useful against *hypogastrium*, the point in the center of the lower abdomen midway between belt line and pubic bone. This is an especially vulnerable spot as it is where all the abdominal muscles meet and leave a hole, just like the whorl of hair at the back crown of the head.

Open-Palm Attack:

Flat, open hand with fingers slightly curved and palm slightly cupped. This formation traps a little air between palm and target area. Since air is practically incompressable, this blow, when used with karate striking technique, is like clouting someone with a handful of rocks.

Striking surface is palm center and fingertips. Remember to keep thumb tight against side of hand. Blow can be delivered with full side-arm swing, or from overhead, snapped down from elbow and wrist like whip. Use against center of chest (breast bone), eye, solar plexus (from side), kidney area, groin (from side or sharply upward), and ear. This is a very destructive shot when employed against an attacker's ear and can be used from very close in.

Base-of-Palm Attack:

This is the most powerful hand blow in the karate arsenal. Imagine holding a length of iron pipe in your hand and thrusting it against an assailant; the base of the palm "hand" is the karate equivalent of this attack.

2. Open palm.

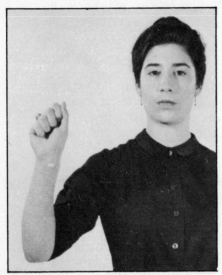

1. Spear hand.

Striking surface is termination of long arm bone at outside base of palm (on line with little finger). Use with hand bent up and formed as in open-palm attack; thrust straight out like punch, or angled up or down to suit target.

Use against center of breast bone, under nose, lower side ribs, temple, or under or over heart. This is a stunning shot and will often cause unconsciousness. Do not wait for results but follow immediately with other shattering karate strikes to nearest exposed target.

Bottom of Fist or Fist Hammer:

Extremely crushing and versatile blow that can be used from any angle from which a hammer, held in the fist, can be used. Striking surface is meaty bottom part of hand when fist is clenched.

Use as follows: Downward: against center of face, left or right collar bone, center of breast bone, temple, and back of neck. Sideward: against solar plexus, groin, side ribs, and kidney area. A life-saving weapon in your hands at all times.

3. Base of palm.

4. Fist hammer.

5. Flat fist.

Flat Fist:

As is evident from the photo, the flat fist (front of regular fist with thumb at side of fingers) presents a striking surface of extreme natural hardness. Except for the front of the forehead it is the hardest bony surface in the body. When snapped down like a whip or striking cobra it is a surprise weapon of crushing power. Use against nose, temple, ear, or breast bone. This is a deadly combination when followed by instant fist-hammer to same spot.

Note: Always wait for attacker to come to you. It is axiomatic that in order to hurt you he must reach out with something to do it. For a brief moment he will be exposed, and it is at precisely this instant that you can dissolve his attack with a surprise series of karate strikes.

HOW TO PRACTICE THE DEADLY KARATE "HANDS"

In order to partake of the health and power-building benefits of karate self-defense it will be necessary to obtain a few pieces of simple equipment.

Tie a rope to a sack containing ten pounds of beans, rice, or peas, and hang from a screw-hook inserted above a doorway. If sack has a rough surface, cover it first with a pillowcase or diaper. When the beanbag is not in use the hook can hold a wind-chime, candle holder, or decorative device. Have the rope long enough so that the beanbag can hang at the level of either head or waist.

Another way to achieve the same results is to lean an ironing board against the wall, flat side out. Take six 12-inch square tatami (grass) mats, usually available in gift shops, and affix to the ironing board at face height. They can be held in place with small clamps, heavy elastic, or one-half inch strips cut from an old inner tube. Where the ironing board touches the wall, it should rest on a couple of cushions or about six inches of foam rubber.

Practicing the Spear Hand:

You are facing ironing board or beanbag. Feet are slightly wider apart than shoulders, toes are pointed slightly in, knees are slightly bent. Do not stiffen up or tense muscles; let weight of body settle into ankles. You are now in basic front stance.

Arms are folded lightly across body, hands hidden behind elbows. You are now in front stance, ready position.

Form spear hand with both hands, and step back on left leg. Weight is even on both feet. Toes still pointed slightly in; knees still slightly bent. You are now in left diagonal stance.

As soon as retreating left leg touches ground, snap left spear hand against center of mat or beanbag.

As left hand goes out right hand is pulled to waist.

As soon as left hand strikes mat return it to waist and thrust right spear hand to center of mat while left hand is still returning.

Now return right hand to waist and refold arms as you advance left foot back to original front stance.

6. Front stance, hands
at side of waist.

7. Front stance, ready
position.

8. Start of circle block
from ready position.

9. Circle block, out.

10. Circle block, up.

11. Circle block,
completed.

Repeat sequence five to ten times.

Now practice from other side of body by retreating right leg (right diagonal stance) and thrusting with right spear hand followed by left spear hand. Use equal number of repetitions.

Note on technique while practicing: Do not attempt to put speed into movements at first. Concentrate on good form as speed will come with good form and practice. Do not attempt to put much power into movements. Stay loose. Work for sharpness and ease of movement. What puts the superpower in Power Karate is form, speed, and practice. *Remember, you only need force for the brief instant that your striking surface is in contact with the assailant.* This karate force will be generated by *form* and *focus.*

Practicing the Open Hand:

Stand in front stance, ready position. Form open palm. Step back on right leg (right diagonal stance). Now imagine you are wearing a blouse with two breast pockets: As you retreat on right leg pull left hand across body until fingers would be under left breast pocket; make half-circle with left arm to height of forehead and finish motion with left hand under right breast pocket. At the same time pull back right elbow until right hand is next to right ear.

Right hand should still be formed into open hand but hanging loosely from wrist. Now whip right hand forward and down like striking cobra to mat, withdrawing left hand to side of waist.

You have just performed a circle block against an assailant's arm that was reaching for your chest or face, and followed it with an open-palm attack to his eye, ear, or breast bone. In a real encounter your assailant is either unconscious or in such pain that he is no longer concerned with either you or his original motives.

Repeat five to ten times with each hand.

NOTES ON TECHNIQUE:

1. *Withdrawal:* Always practice instant withdrawal of striking surface. That is, as soon as your hand makes solid contact with mat or beanbag immediately pull it back from target. Remember, if your hand goes in at 50 miles an hour, bring it out at 60 miles an hour.

2. *Counter movement:* Always move your nonworking arm when striking with your other arm. The exercises in this chapter all include this counter movement. This is the *isometric* principle which keeps you perpetually in balance and ready to block or hit with your spare arm.

16

12. Arm block.

13. Side stance.

14. Forearm block from ready
position, start.

15. Forearm block, completed.

3. *Breathing:* At the moment when your hand touches the target, try breathing out through your mouth. During practice, all in-breaths should be through the nose and all out-breaths through the mouth. A few minutes' practice will make this ancient, healthful breathing pattern automatic. You might try making a little sound on your out-breaths as you hit. The sound can be made aloud or to yourself and will help you concentrate all your energy at the instant of contact. The syllable "HUH" is suggested as it aids in pushing the breath both out and, at the same time, downward into the abdomen in the proper karate manner.

These three principles might be termed the "secret ingredients" which make Power Karate the phenomenally effective system that it is.

Practicing the Base-of-Palm Attack:

Before doing this, practice the following breathing exercise. Stand in front stance with arms at sides. Breathe out through mouth making the HUH sound; release stomach muscles and let air be drawn in through nose. Make out-breath again with HUH. Repeat five to ten times. Increase repetitions with each practice session until you can perform exercise 50 times without tiring.

Now shift mat or beanbag to height of your solar plexus and stand three feet away in front stance, ready position.

Form base-of-palm hand and step forward on left leg (right diagonal stance).

As you step forward sweep left arm diagonally upward as though you are warding off blow (you are) till hand is slightly above height of head.

As left arm goes up, right arm goes to side of waist. The instant this position is achieved thrust right base-of-palm at target. Left hand goes to waist.

Thrust left hand at target as right goes to waist.

Return to front stance and repeat five to ten times.

This is base-of-palm attack with overhead block:

Note: It is often advantageous to block an attacking arm rather than to avoid it by hitting over or under it or sidestepping it. We are therefore introducing blocks into the body of practice material. We know from our teaching experience that these blocking movements are learned much better in action than by memorizing a list of meaningless names. To refresh your understanding, blocks are shown in Figures 7 to 17.

16. Snap block from ready position.

17. Snap block, completed.

18. Front stance, ready position at practice board. Spear hand formed.

19. Right diagonal stance. Left spear hand. . . .

20. Followed by right spear hand.

A block counts as a hit in the karate system and all striking principles apply.

(1) Block sharply. (2) Break off block movement as soon as hard contact is made. (3) Breathe out at instant of contact, and (4) make counter movement with opposite arm.

When a man is blocked he is for a brief instant confused and out of position. In other words, he is open. This is your golden opportunity, so take full advantage of it with karate counters. These counters will be *automatically at your disposal* by observing the practice sequences. Be sure to take full advantage of these fleeting openings, or one may be the last chance of your life to dissolve an assailant's attack.

Practicing Fist Hammer:

Target is at face height. You are in front stance, ready position. Form fist hammer with hands.

Make quarter turn to right by sweeping back right foot and pivoting on left toes.

Left shoulder now points to target and face is turned to left looking at target. You are now in (left) side stance.

As you make turn to side stance, circle both arms across body —left hand making circle block and right hand making counter movement. Arms end up in same position as when you started from ready position except that hands are no longer hidden behind elbows. You have just retreated away from and blocked imaginary hand coming at your face.

Now left hand whips fist hammer across body, striking target with bottom of clenched fist. Right fist goes up alongside ear.

Without lifting feet, pivot left one-quarter turn. You now face target in right diagonal stance.

Bring right hand fist hammer down against target. Left hand goes to side of waist.

Right hand to side of waist.

Advance right leg to front stance.

Repeat five to ten times from each side.

Note: You will have noticed that various stances are being mentioned as you progress in the exercises. The basic stances of Power Karate are very limited in number but, like a ballet dancer's, they give you a wide choice of movement. In a following chapter, on the use of the legs, we will show you how to move from stance to stance with safety, economy, and balance.

The foot diagrams so popular in some purported karate books we

21. Left circle block. Right open palm at ear.

22. Right open palm to mat.

23. Left arm sweep.

24. Right base of palm.

25. Left base of palm.

26. Front stance, ready position, fists formed.

27. Retreats to left side stance, with forearm block.

28. Left fist hammer, right fis at ear.

find to be rarely clear and usually impossible to follow. We prefer to introduce these basic stances with the exercises in the context of block and counter, retreat and advance. In our ancient system of Power Karate it is only the total bodily involvement in the movements that is important.

Practicing the Flat Fist:

Front stance, ready position. Target at face height. Form flat fist. Step back on right leg as left hand snaps up across body to position just above and in front of side of head (upward snap block). Right fist to side of waist.

Strike down and out with left flat fist so that hard front bony surface strikes mat. Keep wrist loose so that hand whips against target. Counter pulls right hand up beside right ear; keep right wrist loose.

Right flat fist whips to target as left goes to side of waist. Return right hand to side of waist. Return to front stance.

Repeat five to ten times from each side.

29. Pivots to right diagonal stance.   **30. Right fist hammer to mat.**

In this above sequence it is the blocking hand which makes the attack. This is the fastest and most effective type of defense although it is not always possible to perform in actual use. Always be prepared to counter with either hand. For example, if in the above situation the left hand was in any way thwarted from countering after the block, the right flat fist cocked at side of waist could be instantly changed to a spear hand and thrust to the attacker's solar plexus.

Some considerations in blocking and striking: All movements must be cohesive but not tense. Hands should be formed but not clenched. *Tense hands and arms only at instant that striking surface contacts target.* Then hand should be withdrawn and unclenched in the same moment. This can be achieved automatically in practice by flexing the hand muscles as you touch the target, unflexing as you withdraw.

This is equally true in blocking since all blocks count as hits. As blocking hand or wrist makes contact—flex; as blocking hand goes on to next motion—relax. This principle of "hard and soft" will protect you in many other ways for reasons that are too deep to examine here.

31. Into Snap Block, right to side of waist.

32. Left flat fist to mat, right to ear.

33. Right flat fist to target.

34. She stands ready in ready position.

35. Steps back with left spear as he moves.

36. Follows up with right spear hand.

37. Circle block. Open palm ready.

38. Block makes opening for open palm.

39. Left arm block.

40. Right base of palm straight in.

41. Left follows right to same spot.

42. She is ready, in ready position.

43. She retreats to side stance with forearm block.

44. Fist hammer to breast bone just after block.

45. Pivots to diagonal stance. . . .

46. As right hammer goes in.

47. Snap block from ready position.　　**48. Left flat fist from block. Right fist at ear.**

When blocking, do not follow the assailant's blocked arm away with your own; this will take you out of position and lose you life-saving time. The sharp karate strike will momentarily neutralize the offending arm—ignore it and go to your next movement.

The same is true if you are attacked with a weapon: club, knife, etc. Do not reach for, but wait for attacker to come to you. Then block and counter and the weapon will have been nullified, because its user is nullified.

When working at the mat or bag always imagine that you are avoiding or blocking a specific blow, grab, or push, and aiming your counter at a specific part of the attacker's body—eye, throat, or temple, for example. Indeed, it would be excellent practice to run through these movements, in good form, with an interested woman friend or member of your own family. You should take turns in attacking and defending. This is of top value both as exercise and in becoming familiar with the movements of an attacking body. Caution should be used and all blows pulled just as light contact is made. We recommend this strongly as one can never be too familiar with the various positions.

The reason we work against a mat or bag, and do not do these exercises solely as a series of freehand movements, is so that you will become used to distancing, timing, and the increasing power of your strikes. Plus the important factor that working against a surface lets you become proficient in the flex-unflex principle at the instant of contact and withdrawal. In this context it should be mentioned that there is no need to have callouses or to ever roughen the hands as in some types of karate.

In fact, due to the stimulation of the tissues and increased blood circulation the skin will be even healthier and softer than when you started this program. This pleasant by-product of your regimen can be hastened by the use of liniment or herbal rubbing medicine at the finish of each session.

Although we do not emphasize powerful block techniques in this system, one further exercise will be of general benefit to your skillful execution of these sequences. Take (left) side stance, ready position. Swing outside of left wrist against target. Right hand goes to waist. Repeat five to ten times. Change to right side stance and repeat. This exercise is designed to build extra facility at blocking skill—in the words of an old saying: "If they can't hit ya', they can't hurt ya'."

49. Right fist follows into same target.

50. Front kick position, with double circle block.

THE BIG GUNS—
FEET, KNEES, AND ELBOWS

Acquiring skill with the legs is like being a general who finds he has an extra army at his disposal when opening a battle.

The legs are instruments of great natural power so our purpose here is to achieve control and focus of this power and learn its skillful application.

The movements used in gaining this skill naturally flush and invigorate the large internal area from the waist down which is so frequently bypassed in most forms of exercise.

The movements emphasize the muscles of the waist and sides and the large muscles of the buttocks, thighs, and hips whose good tone and vigor are so basic to high energy levels and good body function.

We will deal with four fundamental kicking attacks.

Front Kick:

Striking surface is the instep. The kick is snapped up from the knee and is delivered with foot tensed and toe pointed as far down as possible. It is used here, exclusively, to attack the vulnerable groin area of an attacker.

**51. Side-kick stance with forearm
block.**

**52. Front stance, arms at sides,
at practice board. . . .**

Side Kick:

Most powerful of all kicks. Also strikes out farthest distance from body. Striking surface is outside edge of foot. Used with great effect against ankle, shin, knee, and groin.

Ball-of-Foot Kick:

Very handy for breaking up attack and setting up assailant for second and third strikes. Striking surface is ball of foot—hard area behind toes when toes are bent upward. In practicing all kicks it is recommended that the student work barefooted. This is very valuable in timing and distancing as mentioned in the chapter on hand attacks. (In actual use if you are wearing shoes that will protect the toes then kick with the point of the shoe. Otherwise, bend toes upward and deliver kick with area of shoe over ball of foot.) Use against ankle, shin, knee, and groin.

Knee Kick:

Strong kick used in close. Striking surface is bony part of leg just above knee. Practice against bag or mat or pillow tied to under-surface of table. Used mainly against groin, but can be used against

53. Side-kick practice. Start with forearm block from front stance.

54. Side-kick stance, ready to go.

55. Side kick to mat (shin).

56. Diagonal stance, ready to kick. . . .

base of spine, or against abdomen or face if assailant is doubled over from preceding attack.

General note on kicking: Never kick higher than your own waist. No matter how spectacular the high, jumping kicks appear in some karate systems, they dangerously expose the kicker. High kicks take longer to get where they are going, are easier to avoid, and make the leg vulnerable to capture and the kicker to "dumping." Keep your kicks low, as there are plenty of good targets below the belt.

HOW TO PRACTICE POWER KICKING ATTACKS

Front Kick:

Front stance, ready position.

Shift weight onto left leg and slide right foot up along side of left leg as high as knee. Right foot arched and pointed down.

As you raise your right foot bring hands in half-circle across body, stopping in same position as ready position except that hands are no longer hidden behind elbows (double circle block).

Now with foot still arched, snap leg out from knee. Striking surface is bony part of instep between ankle and toes.

Counter motion is hands snapped down to waist. (Just a little practice and you will stop losing your balance.)

If real target is off center, kicking foot may be bent left or right to bear on groin.

Return right leg to front position.

Repeat five to ten times from each side.

Side Kick:

With this powerful kick you have what amounts to a secret weapon in your shoe. The last thing in the world anyone would expect, even a mad fiend, is a side kick to the knee from a poker-faced woman. Learn to control this kick and no one that you can see coming will ever even get near enough to you to hurt you.

Front stance. Arms at sides.

Step back on right foot—turn right toes 90 degrees. (If you start facing front wall right toes should now point to side wall.)

Draw back left leg and raise left foot along right leg to height of right knee. Toes point at ground, knee points forward.

Counter movement is left hand circle block and right hand to side of waist.

Now thrust left leg diagonally downward. As leg goes out turn ankle so that you are striking with upper outside edge of foot.

57. Short left ball-of-foot kick. **58. Diagonal stance with arm block.** **59. Long right ball-of-foot kick.**

Counter movement is jerking both arms forcefully, but keeping them in place.

(Tilt body so that left leg and body make straight line. The higher the final point of the kick, the lower the body.)

Preferred target is the knee, or side of knee, but if attacker is closer to you his shin or ankle are highly effective striking points. Practice side kick at all heights from knee to ankle and later at height of groin.

A side kick to the knee is a disabling attack as it will fracture or dislocate the joint and is also the best single unarmed defense against an attack with weapons, so master it quickly.

Now while still standing on right leg, bring left foot back to side of knee (side kick stance) and repeat kick five to ten times.

Ball-of-Foot Kick:

Front stance; hands at sides. Step forward on left foot (right diagonal stance).

Shift weight to back leg and kick with left foot, snapping kick out from knee.

Counter movement: Form base-of-palm hand and thrust left arm diagonally upward and outward across body (push-away block); right hand to side of waist.

34

60. Stop block stance.

61. Left knee kick.

Bring left foot back to right diagonal stance, shift weight to left foot, and kick out with right foot.

Counter movement is left arm pulled back to side of waist.

Return right foot and repeat five to ten times. Change to right side and repeat five to ten times.

Keep these ball-of-foot kicks low. Theoretical aiming point is just above assailant's ankle. This area is all bone and very susceptible to pain and fracture. As you become more familiar with kicking movements, raise aiming points to middle of shin, knee, and groin. *Knee and groin attacks are disabling kicks when properly delivered.*

Knee Kick:

Front stance, ready position.

Form base-of-palm hand and bring both hands, palms outward, to middle front of chest, about 10 inches from body. (This is stop-block, used to stop attacker who is trying to jump or use his weight against you.) As you perform stop block, step back on right leg, letting most of your body weight settle against right leg.

Release stop block, pulling hands to sides of waist.

As you release stop-block, jerk left knee up sharply to height of your waist.

As soon as you knee-kick, step forward and down with left leg (left diagonal stance) and reform stop-block.

35

62. Stop block stance at board. Rear leg way back to take weight.

63. Front kick stance at board.

64. Front kick to mat.

65. Front kick angled right. . . .

66. And front kick angled left for greater range.

67. Ball-of-foot kick from front.

Bring left knee forward and upward as you release stop-block again and snap hands to side of waist.

Repeat five to ten times. Change sides and repeat again.

Important instruction for all kicking attacks. *Never leave leg dangling after kick.* Either return leg to starting position or stance, or stomp leg forcefully to ground. This will make it impossible to capture your leg and will prevent you from being "dumped" and rendered defenseless.

Kicking is considered a high art among karate enthusiasts. Acquiring skill at the "leg art" is one of the most stimulating, interesting, and graceful aspects of the sport. We have personally observed a woman kick, with great delicacy, a 200-pound practice post across sixteen feet of gym floor with a delightfully exact series of side kicks. None of the men watching could help but offer a shudder of pity for any potential attacker who found himself in range of the lady's foot.

When practicing kicks, observe all principles which apply to hand practice. To wit: Keep loose; flex leg only at instant when striking surface makes hard contact with target.

As soon as firm contact is made, unflex leg and withdraw it with greater speed going back than when it went in. Remember, leg in at 50 miles, leg out at 60 miles.

Concentrate to have all force focused at moment of impact.

Breathe out through mouth at impact point and sound syllable HUH.

These are the karate principles that can break up an assailant's leg and his attack with the proverbial one swift kick.

USE OF THE ELBOWS IN KARATE SELF-DEFENSE

The elbows form a most sturdy line of defense in your body's karate fortress. They can be used with equal facility to the front, back, or side, and even should you miss dead center with your hand shots, the elbows represent formidable obstacles for an assailant to get past—on his way to you.

The striking surface is the bony area one inch below and one inch above the point of the bent arm.

Never strike with the point of the elbow. This is the "funny bone" and will cause as much discomfort to you as to your enemy.

Elbows are naturally hard surfaces, controlled by strong muscles moving on a short arc and offering extremely good leverage. Elbow blows should be delivered flat-footed and sturdily, but with the same in-out speed as the hand weapons.

The target points are many and varied depending on the height, position, and condition of assailant. Main striking points are temple, nose, eye, throat, jaw, under chin, breast bone, side ribs, kidney area, solar plexus, and following the bottom line of the ribs all around the body.

How to Practice the Power Karate Elbow Attacks:

Front stance, ready position. Retreat right leg (right diagonal stance). Left arm stays bent, and moving only from shoulder goes to just above forehead (up block).

Right hand goes to side of waist. Hands are formed into fist hammers.

Without changing angle of arm-bend, move right arm out and up and stop when right fist is by right ear. Target could be solar plexus, breast bone, or point of chin—depending on distance and height of target.

68. Up block, and....

69. Right vertical elbow.

Left arm to side of waist.

Repeat five to ten times from the block position.

The above exercise was for the vertical elbow. The following is for the horizontal elbow, sometimes called the "elbow sweep."

Front stance, ready position. Step back on right leg.

Right arm extends upward and outward across body in diagonal block. Left hand to side of waist.

Sweep left elbow across body until left fist is just in front of right shoulder. Target could be side ribs, solar plexus, kidney area, etc. If arm is swept higher so that left fist finishes movement by right ear then the target would be a vulnerable point in the head or throat.

Right hand to side of waist.

Repeat five to ten times from diagonal block position.

Vertical or Horizontal Elbow, Stepping Forward:

This movement is used to follow up an assailant whom you have opened up and who is trying to recover for a second attack. We will illustrate that with a horizontal elbow.

Front stance, ready position.

Step back on right leg. Right diagonal stance.

Left arm diagonal block. Right hand to side of waist.

Step forward with right leg to left diagonal stance. As you finish forward step, sweep right elbow across front of body.

Left arm to side of waist.

Return to front stance and repeat five to ten times.

Note that elbow attacks work in rapid combination with the fist hammer, so that it would be natural to follow a vertical elbow with a downward fist hammer or a horizontal elbow with a cross fist hammer. By the same token, the elbow is a natural continuation of the fist hammer. We will deal further with these combinations in a following chapter.

In the preceding pages we have presented the fundamental karate principles and defenses. Since one of these basic movements could prove invaluable in a threatening situation, all of them are appropriate to emergency self-defense. If your time is severely limited it would be better to concentrate on learning two or three of the movements exactly and automatically.

One usable defense, at hand when you need it, is worth a hundred half-learned movements.

Even over short periods of time practice builds karate skill and karate skill saves lives.

70. Diagonal block at mat.

71. Right horizontal elbow.

3
WIN!

When the first world conquerer, Alexander the Great, was asked how he went about winning a battle, he replied, "Any way that works." Leo Durocher, the famous Dodger manager, has made the terse comment, "Nice guys don't win ball games," and an equally famous person once said, "Winning isn't everything, but it's so far ahead of whatever's second best, there's no sense talking."

To any person exposed to physical danger these observations apply full force. Any man under attack is in a desperate situation; this is doubly true when the object of the attack is a woman. At the time Power Karate was invented, to lose was to die. After many thousand years we have returned to an era when the perils of our time are nearly as desperate. Therefore, Power Karate holds that there is no substitute for victory—and puts in your hands, or the balls of your feet, the means to win it on the spot.

A man who assaults a woman expects little effective resistance. Consequently he will be off guard to some extent. This small opening advantage combines with the *essential element of surprise* to favor the success of your first defensive blow.

72. Left snap block followed by. . . .

73. Immediate left spear hand.

74. And right spear hand.

75. And left spear hand.

But you cannot stop there. This is the crucial point of your defense and it must be instantly exploited or your life-saving advantage may be gone forever.

Someone has been about to injure or kill you; now that you have momentarily obtained the upper hand, do not stop to render first aid. Instead, go into the opening with every attack you can muster. Your safety lies in that direction. Once you have stunned your opponent you must immediately insure your position; you may never get a second chance.

The Orientals say: He who strikes the first strong blow wins the encounter. What is meant is that he who lands the first shot can get in the second and third; then there is no longer any encounter, because there is no more opponent.

The following sequences will build skill at the essential combinations required for successful self-defense. They are based on the movements taught in the first two chapters. They should be practiced as freehand movements first, then broken down into individual attacks and worked at the home target board.

When practicing as a freehand exercise, remember to keep the movements of the body cohesive and focused. Pull back hand or foot at the instant of contact with imaginary target, move body as a unit, and try to use the Power Karate breathing in rhythm with the movements.

Front stance; ready position.
Right diagonal stance with left snap block; right hand to side of waist.
Left hand spear to high target; right hand jerks in place.
Right hand spear to middle target; left hand to side of waist.
Left hand spear to middle target; right hand to side of waist.

When you have successfully landed the first blow on an offending opponent, one of five things will probably happen.
1. Assailant will stand still and move hands to painful area.
2. Assailant will back up.
3. Assailant will move toward you.
4. Assailant will retreat toward your right.
5. Assailant will retreat toward your left.
The above sequence illustrates how to follow up against an assailant who stands in place. You have blocked his grab and struck the assailant's throat. As he straightens up and his hands go to his throat, you have struck his exposed solar plexus (it could also be his side ribs or groin); as he bends again from the force

76. She waits events in ready position.

77. Retreat to side stance with forearm block.

of the second blow, your left strikes again to his exposed face or neck.

This is a general illustration as you could use other combinations of blocks and attacks. The ensuing sequences are general illustrations for the other probable responses of an attacker.

Front stance; ready position.

Retreat right leg one-quarter turn to (left) side stance. Left hand circle block. Right hand to side of waist.

Left hand fist hammer strikes out across body (like back-hand tennis stroke) to high target.

Slide left foot one-half step; slide right foot one-half step (half-step advance) as left hand comes back to circle block position.

Left hand fist hammer circles up to height of top of head, then strikes down *diagonally* to left side of assailant's face or neck.

Pivot on toes one-quarter turn to left—you are now in right diagonal stance as left hand goes to side of waist and right hand pulls up alongside ear.

Right fist hammer strikes straight down and out to front of assailant's face or chest.

Right hand to side of waist.

78. Left fist hammer instantly after block.

79. Draws left back to ear.

80. Left downward hammer snaps from new direction.

81. Pivots to diagonal stance. . . .

82. And right downward hammer to new target.

Front stance; ready position.

High block, right diagonal stance. Right hand to side of waist.

Right base-of-palm to center target. Left hand to side of waist.

Retreat one full step on left leg (left diagonal stance). Right hand to side of waist.

Left base of palm to high target—under nose or chin. Right base of palm to center target as left goes to side of waist.

Right hand to side of waist.

You will have noticed that these continuations all use the element of change of direction. This tactic is basic to dynamic self-defense.

If the left hand strikes high, the right strikes low; if the right hand comes in from the front, the left strikes from the side; if the first left hand snaps down from overhead the second left hand snaps in diagonally.

From the material you have already mastered, put together other combinations of block and attack movements. Practice them along the stated lines of advance and retreat. In that way you will never have to allow an injured assailant to recover and continue *his* attack against *you*.

Front stance; ready position.

Right diagonal stance with left hand snap block.

Right open palm to ear.

Advance one full step on right leg to right diagonal stance. Left hand to side of waist. Right comes across body to horizontal elbow position.

Back right elbow to high target.

Right diagonal fist hammer to high target.

Right hand to side of waist.

Front stance; hands at sides.

Right high block into right diagonal stance; left hand to side of waist.

Left high block; right hand to side of waist.

Short left ball-of-foot kick; left hand to side of waist.

Long right ball-of-foot kick. Step down on right leg into left diagonal stance.

Right hand base-of-palm to center target. As soon as right base-of-palm lands, circle hand back toward left ear and *chop* down diagonally at high target.

The *chop* is formed by using the edge of the open palm "hand. The deadly combinations can often be used faster in open hand or

83. Middle arm block.

84. Right base of palm.

85. And left base of palm.

86. And right base of palm back to exposed middle.

88. Left open palm whips to ear.

87. Left snap block.

89. As he retreats she advances.

48

90. Back elbow from horizontal elbow position.

91. And downward fist hammer follows elbow.

92. Front stance, arms at sides, waiting.

93. Right arm block stops attack with left. . . .

94. Left arm block stops follow-up right.

95. Short left ball-of-foot kick.

96. Long right ball-of-foot kick.

97. Advances to left diagonal stance with base-of-palm attack.

98. Returns hand to opposite ear.   **99. Cross chop to neck.**

closed hand series. Open hand, for example, would be base-of-palm, open palm, chop; closed hand would be fist hammer, flat fist, or fist hammer, elbow.

The chop can be used in any direction, and to any target, for which the fist hammer is effective. It should be practiced the same way.

In the last self-defense sequence we demonstrated the use of two blocks in a row. Your first block may not always put you in an exact position to counter, so you must calmly await your assailant's next sally. It is also possible that your first blow may not hit "dead center." You must be prepared to block and counter again. If you remain aware that blocks as well as blows can be used in combination, you will always be ready for the unexpected. In this way it will be your assailant who is the victim of surprise and not yourself.

Should you go through life with a gun in your hand, you would use it to defend yourself if attacked. Karate technique puts in your hands much of the power of a pistol at close range—minus the encumbrance, embarrassment, and illegality of going armed. If you were ever forced to actually shoot an assailant in order to save your own life, you would keep your gun ready for your continued protection. If your first shot hit the attacker in the leg you would not stand there defenseless while he limped toward you to renew his attack, but would fire until you were safe. By the same token, learn to use your karate weapons in a series of shots—and win!

100. Stop block, hand snap out. Rear leg takes weight. **101. Release and kick.**

4

HANDS OFF—FOREVER

Alertness, clarity of perception, and quick, precise body responses emerge as some of the side benefits of Power Karate practice. Even a beginner's competence would fortify you with the skill to block or counter anyone who was close enough to grab you. However— although the current state of our society might indicate the need—we do not dwell in an armed camp patrolled by ever-vigilant sentries so it is best to "expect the unexpected." And everyone makes mistakes.

Body grabs are dangerous as once you are bent off balance or lifted off your feet, self-defense becomes increasingly difficult. Response should be immediate, *but do not struggle.* Go almost completely limp; let your body weight settle into your legs and ankles and present a dead weight to your assailant. This will both relax some of his strength and make you more difficult to move. Then seize your opportunity and make the most of it, carrying it through to a safe conclusion.

TYPES OF BODY GRABS

Whether you are grabbed from front, back, or side is of no

102. Eye attack and back step from body grab.

103. Spear hand as soon as possible.

importance. Consider only if your assailant's arms are inside or outside yours.

If your assailant's arms are under yours, attack his eyes.

If your assailant's arms are over yours, attack his groin.

The attack to the eyes should be with the fingertips of the open-palm hand, with the spear hand, or with the thumbs. Dig, press, or strike as hard as you can.

The attack to the groin should be with the spear hand, the base-of-palm hand aimed upwards, or with the entire hand. Dig, strike, or grab and squeeze with all possible snap. If squeezing attack must be used, accompany with strong karate out-breath and mental picture of your fingers closing against your palm.

The purpose of these attacks is to get for yourself a little space in which to work and, if possible, to break the hold.

Attack should be coordinated with a sharp step back to a diagonal stance. (Of course, were you to be grabbed from behind, you would take a sharp step *forward*, then pivot to face assailant.)

As you press, for example, at your assailant's eye, he will free

104. Arms captured with body. Attack groin.

105. Get room for spear hand stab.

106. Captured from rear, attacks fist hammer to groin.

107. Gets space and uses rear elbow.

108. Steps forward from hold and turns with hammer.

one of his hands to defend against yours. At this precise instant you should press hardest and step sharply into diagonal stance. Be sure to snap your attacking hand back with you, so that it doesn't get captured, making you go through another escape routine.

If for any reason the eye or groin are unobtainable as targets. use the following priority of attack points.

If arms are inside assailant's arms:

1. Drive knee into assailant's groin.

2. Bang forehead against assailant's nose or mouth. (This might hurt a little, but is a highly preferable alternative to getting hurt a lot.)

3. Bite assailant's Adam's apple; bite into spot one-half inch below assailant's lower lip; bite assailant's ear. (Biting is an ancient and honorable method of self-defense. Bite hard, force karate breath out mouth, twist head a little, and concentrate on closing teeth. Jaw muscles are surprisingly strong.)

4. Stamp heel against assailant's instep.

If none of these techniques actually break the grip they will win you enough room to get your hands working against assailant's groin.

109. **Finger to neck hollow, from grab with arms trapped at chest.**

110. **Same hand to nose.**

111. **Finishes with base of palm to chest.**

If arms are outside assailant's arms (and you can't get at his eyes) :

1. Attack spot just below Adam's apple and just above collarbone knobs. Be very gentle when testing this on yourself or friends. Use thumb, fingertip, or spear hand. Just push, hard and steady.

2. Strike assailant's ear with open-palm blow.

3. Push or strike under nose with base-of-palm and attack Adam's apple or ear with other hand.

4. Press thumb into spot just below ear and just behind jaw bone.

5. Attack assailant's groin with knee or attack assailant's instep with heel.

6. Use back of vertical elbow (if from behind).

Should you be grabbed by neck with one or two hands from front or rear, waste no time, but instantly dig under assailant's little finger with your first two fingers. Once you get under his little finger, bend it back and snap as sharply as possible; it will break.

This attack to the little finger is also very effective in body grabs from behind, in conjunction with eye-dig. In karate, as in chess or war, you only have to win in one spot.

112. Double open palm to ears and. . . .

113. Down back elbow to breast bone.

114. Into front stance against choke.

115. Forearm block, out.

116. Wrist grab.

117. Snap out with kick.

118. Cross wrist grab.

119. Side stance advance, arm thrust out.

| 120. Push down wrist grab. | 121. Side stance advance snap out. |

DEALING WITH WRIST GRABS

A seized wrist can be either more dangerous or less dangerous than a body grab, depending on your assailant's intentions. Do not take time to inquire.

The instant your wrist is grabbed, simultaneously deliver a karate kick to assailant's knee, shin, or ankle, and snap wrist out of his hand.

If you are close enough, strike at one of your assailant's target points with your free hand as you snap away your captured hand.

Always move your wrist against your captor's thumb, as this is much weaker than his four fingers. Just before you begin your movement, pull your arm very slightly in the opposite direction. If, for example, you are going to escape by snapping and twisting your arm up and out, begin by pulling it in and down about one inch—then let no time elapse before going into escape movement. This trick will cause your assailant to relax his grip in the direction you wish to escape.

Often this twist and snap tactic can be used from a standing position to free the wrist, but be prepared to go right into another sequence if it is unsuccessful.

Never tug or struggle as this will accomplish nothing against a determined assailant. Wrist grabs are potentially quite dangerous and you must exercise much poise and awareness until you have fought free.

122. Double wrist grab.

123. Turning advance break. Wrists go against thumbs.

Should You Be Pulled Forward:

This is one of the reasons that captured wrists are a great impediment, as you can be easily pulled off balance and rendered more or less defenseless. Should you face this situation you must perform the following escape procedure:

1. Step forward faster than you are being pulled. Step either into a diagonal stance or all the way into a side stance, depending on the relative position of assailant.

2. As you advance, keep your arm generally stiff so that the weight of your body is behind it.

3. At the last instant, that is just before your foot touches the ground, lean into it as hard as possible and *snap* wrist against restraining thumb.

4. If this forward movement can be combined with an attack by your free hand or elbow, so much the better.

Although it is difficult to precisely describe the movements involved, an examination of Figures 116 to 128 and just a little practice with a friend, will make these escapes exact, accurate, and dependable.

124. Two hands grab one.

125. Eye attack.

126. Cross grab.

127. Arm up to attack.

128. Retreat, attack wrist, and snap out.

Should Assailant Move Toward You:

Use (1) reverse motion trick by pushing arm slightly *toward* him before snapping it back and (2) step back into diagonal stance as you free wrist.

Attacking Assailant's Wrist:

Another excellent way to free a captured wrist is to crack your own wrist against attacker's wrist as you snap away your captured arm. This should be combined with retreat to side or diagonal stance. The success of this method is greatly reinforced by practice of blocking exercise against home target board as described at end of Chapter 1.

Some of the desired responses, such as biting or eye attack, may seem unusually harsh. But the events which caused a book of this nature to be prepared were not the random wolf-whistles of exuberant school boys, but the repeated onslaughts of psychopathic sadists whose intentions are best left unprobed. The authors believe it is a far more rational course to have these life-saving responses at your disposal and never need them, than to be in a situation where your person is endangered and not know how to react.

The completion of any of these escape methods will leave your assailant readily exposed to your deadly karate counter blows; use them hard, fast, and often.

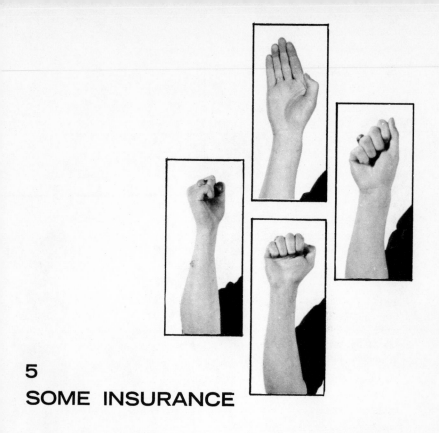

5
SOME INSURANCE

All successful combats are characterized by large measures of surprise, trickery, and deceit. Whether the encounter is between animals, armies, or individuals, this principle is a rule of life and, therefore, survival.

Always expect the unexpected, and be prepared for the sudden lunge, rush, or grab. A potential assailant can be just as dangerous when he starts to smile, as when he stops.

The following information will help you in coping with threatening situations of a general nature, using Power Karate principles. The assumption here is that you will be attacked.

Under no circumstance should you fight if there is any other course of action open to you, if there is any help available, if there is any other alternative available. If, however, you are forced to use Power Karate in your own defense, *give it everything you've got, and follow through to a safe conclusion.*

Note: Never attempt to employ a weapon: gun, knife, club, etc., unless you are thoroughly familiar with its use, as you could be easily disarmed and have the weapon turned against you.

129. Under certain attack she appears terror stricken.

130. His eyes stay on her hands as leg goes up.

Aspects of Ready Position:

This position helps you face a potential attacker, completely ready to defend yourself, without appearing either prepared or belligerent. Thereby, you will not put him on guard and make his attack more difficult to defend against.

If he comes toward you, back up by stepping back into diagonal stance, front stance, diagonal stance, etc. Try not to change expression, or betray nervousness. Do not think about or concern yourself with outcome of encounter, only about your next response. Ready position helps you stay "together" by hiding hands and keeping arms in relaxed, but fixed position.

If assailant begins to circle you, alter stance by half-steps so as to continue facing him.

Ready position gives assailant no "handle" on you: nothing to grab or pull, no emotional display to guide or incite him. (Not all, but many would-be attackers have been out-faced by a display of confident calmness.)

In order for an assailant to hurt you he must reach out to do it. This is the moment you must watch for; it is at this instant that he is out of position and exposed to your block or deadly counter.

Should assailant back you into a corner, it will become necessary for you to initiate the attack. Try to smile or say something disarming and kick to his shin or ankle area; follow immediately with block and/or hand attack to new target. This can be accomplished either from front stance or while stepping into diagonal stance. Kick with back leg as soon as front leg touches ground.

It would be excellent technique if you could yell in conjunction with this movement. Use karate out-breath and yell "HUH" as loud as possible. Kick on the noise. The shock of a good karate yell will momentarily paralyze an assailant. Turn home radio up and practice this occasionally with kicking or striking movement.

If you are rushed, use stop-block and knee kick sequence (see Chapter 2).

Don't-Hit-Me Position:

This is essentially a side-kick position combined with a little acting ability.

A frequent category of attack situation is when someone is walking forcefully toward you. You are not certain of his motives but you are alone and feel it unwise to let him approach you too closely.

131. Pow! Side kick breaks knee.

**132. She waits, looking friendly.
Spear hand is formed.**

**133. Fast spear hand
ends encounter.**

When assailant is three to four feet away, perform the following sequence of movements.

1. Raise both arms slowly overhead, right arm slightly higher than left, fingers spread and bent, palms outward.

2. Face should assume the most fearful, terror-stricken expression imaginable; open and close mouth as if trying to speak and keep working and twisting lower lip. Try to look like the innocent girl in all the horror films at the instant before the thing from the lagoon clamps his slimy hand on her neck.

3. As hands go above head, step back into right diagonal stance: slide back left leg until it touches right foot, then raise it to side-kick position.

4. As soon as assailant is in range, pivot forward on right toes and snap side kick to his nearest knee.

As bizarre as this instruction may sound, it is considered an extremely effective tactic, and is the favorite defense of professional bouncers when faced by an angry patron wielding a bottle or bar stool.

The maneuver is based on two very sound principles. The first is that given any group of moving objects the eye will tend to

134. Have mercy.

135. Diagonal stance and base of palm.

136. She has no mercy.

follow the highest among them. Thus, between your face and hands the assailant's attention is well misdirected from your foot. The second, more essential, principle is that with a proper side kick you can break an assailant's knee when he is still fully twelve inches too far away to touch you with his hand.

Try this with a friend. Set up the side kick. You will see that when the edge of your kicking foot is resting against his knee, his outstretched hand will be a good distance from your face or body.

If you are wearing high-heel shoes, make the striking surface the point of your heel as this will give you even greater reach. Should the shoe break or come off rid yourself quickly of the other shoe and continue your defense. This is one of the reasons we recommend occasional kick practice while barefooted.

The Have-Mercy Position:

In the event that you are caught in a corner or against a wall, or are suddenly grabbed from close up by your clothing, hair, or upper arm, perform the following movement:

Bring hands up under chin, elbows against sides. Hands can be either loosely clenched or pressed palms together as if praying.

Try to express fear and pleading with face and wait for next development.

The instant assailant moves, lash out with hand to face or neck target. This should be done whether he moves his hand, leg, or simply shifts his body position.

The winning principle involved here is that by having the hands together in the center of the body *you can strike your assailant in a much shorter line than he can strike you.*

His face and neck are eminently vulnerable to your spear-hand, base-of-palm, or chop attack. If you just wait to take advantage of the slight distraction of his movement, he will not be able to block your attack. Your facial entreaty and the disguised, pleading appearance of your hands will sufficiently mask the fact that you are waiting your chance, hands at-the-ready, for a life-saving slash to his Adam's apple.

In case you are struck, don't give up automatically. We have all paid sufficient visits to the dentist to know that one does not perish from a little pain. And, as a general rule, a man does not strike a woman with the same kind of unconscious force he would use in striking another man. Do not finger the spot where you are struck; do not stand around waiting to see how much it will hurt. Instead, lash out immediately, preferably with a karate kick, and your assailant will have a little something of his own to think about.

In the serious circumstance that you are confronted by more than one attacker (1) don't faint and (2) don't surrender.

Concentrate your attention on the person closest to you, ready to use all the karate information you have mastered. Then worry about the second or third assailant. It is an encouraging fact that many a gang attack has dissolved at the sight of a little blood or the sound of some pain issuing from the leader.

These may seem rather disturbing observations with which to end this section, but it is the author's firm belief that one's deepest fears can be overcome by dealing with them and learning to master them.

A young Eurasian girl was recently attacked by two punks on a dark street in San Diego. Relying on her knowledge of Power Karate she walked away from the situation—and they didn't.

Avoid lonely spots and do not seek out situations where you can get in trouble, but once confronted *explode with every weapon at your command.*

There is a lot of hope.

PART 2

KARATE PRACTICE TECHNIQUES FOR FAMILY PROTECTION

137. Base of palm and push block.

138. Left base of palm and block.

139. Advance attack and block.

6

PREPARING A KARATE POWER
BASE WITH PARTNER

Our interests often prove more pleasant when pursued in company. To this end we have prepared a unique section of karate information that can be practiced to excellent purpose by family or friends. Not only women, but men, boys, and teen-agers will discover much that is of value to the body, spirit, and sense of well-being in the ensuing pages.

Some of the material will augment your skill by adding depth and scope to the ideas presented in the first section; while new techniques will create a wider dimension of safety and flexibility to your defense potential, should you ever be forced to invoke it.

Our first dual practice technique is frequently used as a warm-up exercise in karate classes—where large groups of men and women sign up for self-defense instruction that usually runs about ten dollars a lesson. The students pair off to perform the movement, generally called "karate across the floor."

In this procedure, the partners begin by facing each other a little less than arm's length apart.

140. Power practice for side kick.

141. Side kick and leg retreat.

144. Turning into next side kick.

145. Going into side kick stance.

142. Advance from side kick.

143. Next side kick and retreat.

146. Final kick and retreat.

One partner advances with a striking movement that stops just short of the target, while the other partner retreats with a blocking movement that stops just short of contact.

At the finish of the sequence (see Figures 137 to 156) the retreating partner now advances, and the advancing partner now retreats and blocks.

Note: These are the only karate exercises in which the movements are not done with a snap and release.

In this exercise all movements of the arms and legs, by both partners, are performed slowly and uniformly, as if the limbs were pushing against a heavy resistance.

For full effect this principle must be applied to the counter movement, as well as to the striking and blocking.

Practice at "distancing" and acquiring the "feel" of another person in striking and blocking are the partial functions of this type of exercise. Its main purpose, however, is in laying the foundation for a tremendous base of power for use in an actual encounter. The studied tension in the muscle movement is akin to charging one's batteries should a real jolt ever be needed in serious self-defense.

Here again, by the way, is represented the *isometric* principle in Power Karate. There is no other work-out system that can flush and refresh both the external and deep internal muscles of the body as fully and in as brief a time as the movements offered in this chapter. No matter what type of exercise you may be used to, you will begin immediately to feel the effects of these. We would like to cite this as another testament to the wisdom of the ancient peaceful monks of High Asia who invented Power Karate.

147. Elbow attack and push block.

148. Fist hammer after elbow.

149. Advance and retreat.

150. Ready to strike and block.

152. Pivots and continues with right hammer.

151. Cross fist hammer and defense.

153. Start of kick and retreat.

154. Continuation of kick.

155. Into diagonal stance and spear hand.

156. And next spear hand and block.

7
BODY CONTACT

Since there is no substitute for experience, light contact practice is deemed essential for complete karate protection. The know-how gained from brief periods of freehand blocking and striking will reveal much about the demeanor of an attacking individual. These insights form a broad measure of protection between yourself and a surprise attack. Once you become familiar with the modes and attitudes that invariably precede an aggressive movement, it will be most unlikely that anyone can ever get the "jump" on you.

This type of exercise will insure your own precision at emergency self-defense, as moving, blocking, and striking will become habitual and automatic. There should be no intervening period of thought between an aggressive gesture and your own defensive response. Contact practice will eliminate the lag, and, moreover, help you tell the true from the false. That is, you will instantly perceive the difference between a threat or feint and an actual onslaught, requiring your own devastating answer.

To practice this method the training partners face each other at arm's length. One is the "attacker"; the other one "defends." The attacker endeavors through various karate stances and "hands" to work in close enough to fool and strike the defender. The defender simply defends, and attempts to strike after blocking.

Of course, by striking we mean a light touch to the target area. All counters must be "pulled," stopping just at the surface of the body. In this way the exercises are a lot of fun, and no one is ever hurt.

Practice in the first week should consist only of hand attacks and hand counters.

The second week should emphasize leg attacks with leg counters.

The third week should practice leg attacks with hand counters.

After this, all attacks and counters can be interchanged into free-movement exercise.

When the attacker has landed twice, or when the defender has countered twice, the roles should be reversed.

If the group is to receive the full benefit of this practice, the aggressor must continually carry the attack to the defender. Otherwise, the sets become too static.

Naturally, if the defender sees or senses an opening he should attempt to take advantage of it. Since karate is essentially the art of the counterattack, it is always assumed in these freehand exercises that the aggressor will lose.

Note that the defender should hold the blocks till the last possible instant. The further the attacker's arm or leg extends from his body, the more he is out of position; thus, the defender's block has far greater effect in opening the way for his counter.

A good rule is: Never reach. If after blocking, an attacker is too far away for you to strike, either (1) break off the action or (2) use one of the advances to close with him and take advantage of any positional weakness.

If there is a good opening to the eyes or throat, and you can reach out slowly, and in full control, to touch near the target area, then this is quite safe. Otherwise, we never attack to these two targets in practice.

As you gain competence in this exciting form of contact exercise, you will be pleased with the logical evolutions of movement that occur. The experience is of immense importance to your own emergency defense potential. Although karate contains a wide repertoire of techniques, the logic of an actual attack is fairly rigid. You will soon know, without thinking, what you can and can't do from any given position.

If you are ever beset by an unfriendly attacker, your "muscle knowledge" will tell you what both he and you can do before he knows what is happening. As has been proved many times in the past, this will work to an attacker's permanent disadvantage, and the assurance of your own safety.

157. Palm block and
diagonal stance.

158. Immediate back
hand to target.

8

A BASIC DEFENSE FOR WOMEN, CHILDREN, AND MEN

Naturally, the children of the household will be eager to join with any group karate activity. Between the boys' magnet of combat and a girl's delight in graceful movement, it would be difficult if not impossible to stop the rush. Even if it were possible, they should not be discouraged as the experience of all karate instructors is that children, of either sex, are far and away the best students. Saturday afternoon *dojos* are swamped with boys and girls from six to sixteen eagerly performing their fascinating health- and confidence-building karate exercises.

One should never hesitate to include children in this highly moral and spiritual form of physical movement. Any tool can be improperly used, but it is far less likely to occur when the child is taught the use of this tool by a respected adult. Karate knowledge, sometimes unethically presented, is available in any book store, so it is far better to offer it honestly in the good and familiar environment of the home.

Once the difference is pointed out between a normal situation,

159. Palm block, fist.

160. Back fist right after block.

such as a simple challenge, and a serious situation, such as being jumped by a marauding gang or being grabbed by a sex pervert, the youngster can deal with his daily encounters as well as anyone else. In fact, it has been demonstrated that the karate-trained child gets into fewer fights because his confidence makes him less sensitive to teasing and unimportant threats.

In the face of a serious episode, any boy will gleefully let fly with his karate power against the assault of a child-molester, and will no doubt fight free or gain the margin of time needed for escape or adult help. Using the element of surprise and the child's uncluttered muscular reflexes, even a young girl has a first-rate chance to save herself from this most disturbing aspect of our current social decay. Speaking as a parent, the author highly prefers the idea of a brief and successful violence to the all-too-frequently reported ritual of assault, trauma, and even worse finale of these ever-increasing incidents.

All material in this volume is valid and effective for children. If you have not started with the first chapter, here is a handy method for introducing a youngster to the excitement of Power Karate—and an important addition to the defensive capability of everyone. It is called the three-hand exercise.

First we must add two more "hands" to our karate arsenal.

We have already learned two surfaces of the fist, the fist hammer and the flat fist, and two surfaces of the open hand, the chop and the open palm (see "hand" photos in Chapter 1). We will now include the back fist and the finger whip.

Back Fist:

Striking surface is the back of the closed fist in the area just below the two large knuckles. The back fist can be used downward (from beside ear), diagonally downward (from across body), backhand (from across body), and diagonally upward. It can, in other words, be used in all directions of the fist hammer. Target areas are face, neck, and temple, solar plexus, under heart, kidney area, and groin. When held by ear, hand should hang loosely from wrist and be whipped to target as in open-palm attack.

Finger Whip:

Striking surface is back surface of fingers when hand is open. The finger whip is used diagonally or from overhead, and is snapped as in open-palm attack. Target area is nose and eyes. The idea of the finger whip is not to stun or even injure your assailant. The snapping, whip-like contact of the hard back surface of your fingers to his face will break up his attack, and will disconcert your assailant sufficiently to pave the way for your second counter.

Practicing the Three-Hand Exercises:

Face home target board in front position, hands at sides.

Step back to right diagonal stance. Left hand to side of waist; right hand open-palm block (hand circles upward across body and face—blocking an imaginary arm, wrist to wrist).

Strike target with finger whip.

Repeat from front position and strike target with chop.

Repeat from front position and strike target with open palm.

Repeat from left side.

Begin sequence again, striking with back fist.

Repeat with fist hammer.

Repeat with flat fist.

Repeat from left side.

Now take your striking mat and lay it on a sturdy table top.

Stand in front position with hands at side of waist. Without moving feet, do the open-palm block and run through the three open-hand and three closed-hand sequences.

Strike downward at target mat on top of table. In this form of the exercise you can go for power. Breathe out and withdraw hand at instant of contact. Fist hammer, chop, and back fist are tremendously strong weapons and can render spectacular damage to an assailant. This is the method that karate demonstrators, who break bricks and huge thicknesses of wood, train with to exhibit those incredible feats. Of course, it is wise to go a little easy at first, until the striking surfaces become accustomed to the mat.

With a mastery of the three-hand exercises you should never be liable to surprise attack. *No matter what the direction of the thrust to your face, head, or upper body, you will have a reflex (open palm) block in action. Then, no matter how your hand is formed or in what position it ends up, you will have an automatic counterattack to your exposed assailant.*

161. Palm block start, from ready position.

162. Palm block, up.

163. Palm block completed.

164. Palm block to side.

165. Palm block against attack.

166. Instant base of palm to heart.

167. Palm block closer in.

168. Spear hand from block.

169. Start palm block sequence at table.

170. Back hand to mat.

171. Chop to mat.

172. Open palm to mat.

Try the three-hand movements with a partner. Run through the open-hand and closed-hand sequences. First practice by stepping back into a diagonal stance, then stand further from your partner and step forward into a diagonal stance.

When you have become familiar with the movements and distancing, practice the sequence while moving forward and backward across the floor with partner. Have partner direct a series of right and left "round-house" attacks to your head.

Retreat to right diagonal stance, open palm block, right hand whip.

Retreat to left diagonal stance, open palm block, left hand whip.

Retreat to right diagonal stance, open palm block, right chop.

Retreat to left diagonal stance, open palm block, left chop.

Practice all six hands in this manner; then reverse the movement and run the hands while advancing. Remember, the block and counter are two distinct movements. Never "spill" one into the other. Step back and block; the instant the block is solid, strike with the counter.

As a final polish for this basic and essential defense tactic, follow each strike with a second attack by hand, elbow, or kick. You will soon see how vulnerable any of the three-hand counters can leave a surprised assailant.

The counterbalance for all of these movements is to jerk the opposite hand in place at the waist.

Do not be concerned by the varying sizes of the members of your family participating in your karate activity. In group karate classes, the height of the man may run from five feet two inches to six feet six inches. The men pair off in round-robin fashion and differences in height, speed, and reach always cancel out with the acquisition of karate technique. Many respected instructors, holders of advanced belts, stand less than five feet tall. It is very advantageous to practice with people of varying heights and weights, as one is never in a position to choose or predict the size of an assailant.

173. Palm block, fist.

174. Back fist to mat.

175. Fist hammer to mat.

176. Flat fist to mat.

9

A 30-DAY CRASH PROGRAM FOR FAMILY SELF-DEFENSE

Karate basics can be practiced any place, any time. You can form a karate "hand" when opening a swinging door. You can do karate breathing to calm the nerves or relax the stomach at any point during the day or night. In fact, a regular series of karate breaths upon retiring is an excellent method of achieving quick, calm sleep, without side effects or pill hangovers. You can practice up-blocks or snap-blocks while soaping yourself in the shower. As you become familiar with the material many short, beneficial procedures will come to you.

If, however, the unfortunate fact of physical assault in our society is to be met with firmness, immediacy, and success, a crash program of routine practice is of the highest order of priority.

A few minutes a day, a few days a week, can well be the difference between life and death.

After the very first day you will be equipped with a killing weapon in either hand, prepared to offer a deadly counterthrust to the neck of a destruction-bent assailant.

A week's practice will give scope, flexibility, and competence to your skill.

At the end of a month you will be soundly versed in the fundamentals of an unbeatable system of karate self-defense, secure in your capacity to cope with the most sudden and appalling of threats.

The month passes anyway. What better way to spend it than in the healthy pursuit of your own survival?

Whether in a small, cleared area of your apartment kitchen or in a family recreation room, elaborately equipped, your first month's practice should proceed by the following schedule.

First Session:

Warm up by doing karate breathing while standing in front stance, ready position.

Breathe in through nose and out through mouth, forcing some air into lower abdomen. On in-breath let air be sucked down into lower abdomen.

Be sure that body is balanced in front stance: Feet parallel; head and back in straight line to ground; shoulders at equal height.

First five minutes: Practice spear hand, open palm, and fist hammer at home target board (sequences in Chapter 1).

Second five minutes: Practice three-hand exercises at target board (Chapter 8).

Third five minutes: Practice three-hand exercises and finger-spear sequence with partner.

Second Session:

Warm up.

First five minutes: Practice finger spear, base of palm, and flat fist at target board.

Second five minutes: Practice these three sequences with partner.

Third five minutes: Practice three-hand exercises at target board.

Third Session:

Warm up.

First five minutes: Run all five "hands" at target board. Work on sharpness of movement.

Second five minutes: Practice three-hand exercises with mat or beanbag on table top.

Third five minutes: Have partner throw light karate hands

while you defend by mixing sequences from Chapter 1 with three-hand block and counters.

Second Week:

First session: Become familiar with leg defenses by practicing ten minutes free kicking sequences (Chapter 2). Finish with five-hand and three-hand sequences at target board.

Second session: Ten minutes kicking practice with partner. Partner should stand just out of range and move forward or back as dictated by kick sequences.

Five minutes of elbow attack practice at target board.

Third session: Five minutes kicking practice at padded target board.

Five minutes elbow attack practice at target board.

Five minutes mixed leg and elbow practice with partner.

Third Week:

First session: Ten minutes of hand sequences at target board. Five minutes power-base practice (Chapter 6) with partner.

Second session: Ten minutes kicking practice at cushioned target board.

Five minutes power-base practice with partner.

Third session: Ten minutes elbow-attack practice at target board.

Five minutes power-base practice with partner.

Fourth Week:

First session: Ten minutes freehand combination sequences (Chapter 3).

Five minutes body contact practice (Chapter 7).

Second session: Ten minutes escapes and breaks (Chapter 4).

Five minutes body contact.

Third session: Five minutes escapes and breaks.

Five minutes combination practice broken down at target board.

Five minutes body contact practice.

Fourth session: Five minutes three-hand exercise on table top.

Five minutes combination practice—broken sequences at target board.

Five minutes body contact.

You are now prepared to meet nearly any attack situation. Your level of skill and sharpness can be maintained by fifteen minutes per week of Power Karate practice.

If you wish to reinforce your ability and to deepen and expand your areas of good health, body tone, and karate acuteness, continue on a three-a-week schedule. Break down workouts as above and always concentrate on those techniques in which you feel least adept. In this way, you will generate a continuing progression of greater and greater abilities.

All methods in this section can be practiced by a single individual, with the exception of body contact and blocking practice. This gap can be filled with the occasional aid of an interested friend, or by making up and responding to an imaginary attack situation—in the way that a prize fighter "shadow boxes."

People generally practice karate in the company of a partner or family group. If your own group is large have one section do one thing, blocking practice for example, while another section performs another, say sequences at target board. In this way the workout time will be used efficiently and there will be no dead spots.

It is suggested, however, that time permitting, all participants observe body contact practice, as so much karate knowledge can be absorbed by observing others in action, that it is well worth the few extra minutes.

At all times, make the goal of your karate exercises focus toward a further exactness of movement. This is the single quality that dictates victory. It only takes the first block and counter to determine your success.

If your work in the emergency basics of self-defense has excited your interest in Power Karate as a bodily art, then by all means proceed to the information in the third section of this book. Here you will encounter the ancient and brilliantly efficient defense secrets of the finger-tip attack and special advanced training procedures, plus many more examples of the "ancient unbeatable art."

The following section contains information which will be new to the enthusiast and stimulating to the beginner.

Treat yourself to the varied benefits of skillful karate—you might need it.

PART 3

KARATE IN ITS ULTIMATE USE

10
THE IMPREGNABLE POSITION

The basic karate defensive position is based on ancient principles of Oriental warfare. It combines apparent vulnerability with a potential for instant deadly retaliation. This position can lure your opponent to place himself in such an exposed position that he will fall instant victim to your karate block and counter. The hard block and swift counter form the essence of karate. As you advance, with practice, you will be able, in many instances, to eliminate the block —relying on your practiced karate reflexes to avoid the attack, at the same time placing yourself in the proper position to rain deadly karate counters to your opponent's exposed areas. The basic defensive position is as follows (see Figure 177):

Feet apart, slightly wider than shoulder width with weight mostly on back leg, side to opponent, to present a smaller target; right hand, *fist up*, cocked at side of waist; left forearm, elbow high, forms a protective bar across forehead, just above the eyebrows; fist, fingers down, slightly rotated out.

Rear foot instep toward opponent, front foot toes toward opponent. The front hand acts as a cleaver, protecting you from any blow

177. Basic defense position.　　　　　**178. BDP with snapping chop block.**

that may be thrown, from the top of the head to the groin. The right hand stays cocked as a surprise counter. The offensive and defensive use of the feet will be explored in another chapter.

The first thing to be practiced after achieving the basic defensive position is the downward chopping motion of the left hand. Always remember—*self-defense begins with the block.* The defensive chop (which, after conditioning, is capable of breaking an attacker's arm) is snapped down sharply from the elbow, without moving the shoulder. Elbow stays bent and high in relation to the hand. Remember, wait for the blow—do not reach for it.

The power for the blow does not come from any movement of the shoulder—rather it is whipped and snapped downward sharply from the elbow joint. The shoulder only moves to adjust the height of the elbow for blows below the waist. It is unnecessary to lower the shoulder or elbow at all for blows above the waist, as this position will protect you from top of head to waist with no movement except the snapping chop block from the elbow. This is an excellent defensive position as it provides an absolute economy of movement on your part, and requires a great amount of exposure to your opponent, especially exposure to his very vulnerably extended arm. Keep in mind that your snapping chop block is also a hit, which not only protects you from attack and leaves your opponent seriously

179. BDP, low chop block.   **180. BDP, forearm block.**

out of position, but which with practice will enable you at the same time to fracture or disable the attacking arm. Aim for the spot on the thumb side of the forearm about an inch above the wrist.

For blows aimed at you from the waist to the knee the same basic position is maintained, and the same block used. It becomes, however, necessary to adjust the height of the shoulder to reach the attacking arm or leg. Remember—do not hit from the shoulder, but at all times maintain the angle of the arm, and deliver the block in snapping, chopping fashion, sprung from the elbow. In time, and with practice, you will be able to break or disable a leg, because a kick dangerously exposes the knee, shin, and ankle of the attacker.

In practice, try first for skill and speed in blocking, then, gradually, for concentration of power in the blocking hand.

In a combat situation maintain this position at all times, as a boxer would maintain his basic stance, and at the same time, keep moving relative to your opponent.

This is your basic position. As you progress in your karate training, you will learn other tested positions to facilitate your karate defense-attack. However, this will always remain your basic and emergency position. In this position, with properly trained hands and feet, and your back against a wall, you will present a relatively invulnerable front to even a group of attackers. You will be set for lightning defense and attack, and they will think twice before attempting to penetrate your unusual and frightening position.

Remember—once you have blocked. your opponent is exposed. This is the time when your karate counters will be most telling. Reply instantly to the opening that your opponent's blow and your block have created.

Be alert. Do not reach. Keep moving. Wait for the blow to come to you. You will know, in practice, that you are blocking too soon, and reaching, if your block lands on your partner's forearm instead of on his wrist. It is less effective as a block. and is potentially dangerous as it will enable a clever opponent to feint you out of position. Eliminate all bad habits in practice right at the beginning. Remember—the essence of karate is to draw your opponent out of position, and not to be faked out of *your* position. When you are out of position you are not only open, but committed to a predictable course of action. Even the best boxers have always been counterpunchers. It is always easier for a trained man to perceive the direction of an attack and counter it from a flexible position, than to change an already started action. Bullfighting is based on this idea. The bull must be faked into the first move. Once the bullfighter sees the nature and direction of the attack, he may then control or avoid the movement. Were it the other way around, there would be many bulls and no bullfighters.

181. BDP, right high arm block.

182. BDP, right low chop block.

11
THE FIST: SUPER POWER!

Man's clenched fist historically has always been the symbol of aggressive violence. It is a primary weapon. It combines the tremendous power potential of a hard surface with shortness of delivery, and because it is thrown in a straight line, preferably in a slightly downward direction, it is extremely difficult to block. With karate hand conditioning, and the secrets of the karate striking technique, your fist blow can become in fact a battering ram—the true *one-punch* weapon that ends the encounter. Even the small, light-weight man can obtain the *one-punch* power that is decisive in all combat. By conditioning the natural hard surface of the fist with karate conditioning and training, you not only will forge a one-shot knockout blow, but will have, in addition, a weapon capable of stunning, and breaking bone wherever it lands. Karate masters, with the *naked fist*, are able to break two or more bricks, and one has recently, in a public demonstration, killed a charging bull with a single karate punch.

Steady karate training will enable you, too, to generate this kind of explosive karate power. But even should you never wish to break a brick or publicly display your punching strength on a wild animal, you can still achieve a surprisingly sturdy punch, sufficient to stun the strongest opponent, after only a very short period of karate training. By concentrating on sharpness, focus of power, instant withdrawal, proper stance, hand conditioning, perfect karate breathing, and the other ancient techniques to be explained in this chapter on the fist-ram, you will be pleasantly shocked at how quickly you will feel the deep surge of sharp, hard, one-punch, karate knockdown power.

The fist-ram is trained and executed as follows: Stand one pace from the mat in the basic defensive position. Be sure the right fist is cocked, palm up, *at* the waist. Block imaginary round-house right to head with upward snapping chop of the left hand. Immediately counter with right fist to the middle of the mat. As soon as you have made contact with the mat, immediately withdraw your fist to the original position. This technique of instant withdrawal is the bedrock of the ancient system of karate fighting. Instead of putting time-wasting strength into a follow-through, a quick withdrawal of the hand converts the wasted energy of the follow-through into focused power at the instant of hitting. It is this secret that enables light-weight men to throw harder punches than the strongest of fighters. In addition, the instant withdrawal enables you to be back in position and ready to move with further blocks and counters. When your opponent throws his long punch, with follow-through, he is committed to a course of action, which, as mentioned previously, weakens him. As you are prepared to speedily recall your blow, should it miss or be blocked, you are ready to return to a position which is not only less vulnerable than your opponent's but one which allows you to quickly capitalize upon his errors.

Concentrate on pulling the punch back even faster than it goes forward. Somehow, the energy of the blow is concentrated into the instant of impact, giving you more than double power for each blow. This is the principle discovered by the ancient masters, and the *true* secret of karate superhitting power. Practice it until it is as automatic as are all of your hits, chops, pokes, and kicks.

The fist-ram fist, tightly clenched, always starts finger-side up. As the fist moves forward begin rotating it downward into regular fist position. Just before impact it should have completed its turn, so that the fingers are now down. Now, reverse the procedure on withdrawal. It is important to remember not to bend the wrist. Keep it straight, neither up nor down in relation to the forearm.

Now, after you have done your chop-block, and your right hand

183. Left fist at practice post.

184. Right fist to high target.

is speeding toward the mat, the left hand should be returned to the basic defense position, or dropped and cocked at the side of the waist, *simultaneously* with the forward movement of the fist-ram.

Your choice of positioning of the left hand, in combat, would depend on the actual situation. Practice both ways.

For the left hand: Begin in basic defense position, one pace from mat. Imagine a low hook or high kick to your right side. Chop down and out with a snapping motion with your right hand; at the same time drop left hand to cocked position at the side of the waist. Return right hand to side of waist, simultaneously countering with left fist-ram to middle of mat. Once punch has landed, concentrate on same instant withdrawal.

Always begin practice for either hand from the described positions so that the blocks and counters will become automatic. By practicing this daily, your defense to various blows will become automatic, and as the man who does not have to think in combat,

185. Snap block, ready for left fist or right hammer.

186. Forearm block against fist.

187. Followed by fist to exposed side.

but can react reflexively to a specific attack, has an overwhelming advantage, you will already have benefited immeasurably from your stationary practice.

You should work up to 100 repetitions in series of 10 or 20 with each hand after the initial blocking sequence ending in a punch; hold your position and repeat the punch for 10 or 20 repetitions. Then change hands.

There are several effective variations of this basic combination of block and punch. It can be done as described above should your opponent be advancing toward you; should he retreat after the block, practice stepping forward on the right foot as you throw the long fist-ram; should you perceive and penetrate the nature of the attack step forward with the block, followed in the same way with the fist-ram counter.

Practice all three variations.

In conditioning the fist against the mat, keep in mind the Oriental adage: "Climb a mountain slowly, and you will reach the peak." In other words, take it easy—don't injure your fist, it will only impede your progress. On the other hand, work as hard as you can. Try for sharpness and accuracy until your skin and bone become sufficiently toughened for you to let out your steadily increasing karate power. Cut hands heal slowly; soft hands cannot deliver power. Work hard, but only as hard as you have to. As they say in Okinawa, "To master anything great, you must hurt yourself a little."

12

FINGER-TIP SPEAR—
THE ULTIMATE WEAPON

When the ancient monks, in their efforts to protect themselves and the peasants around their monasteries from the depredations of armed brigands, cast their eyes on the fighting arsenal of the bandits, in an effort to equal the fighting power of armed men while still barehanded, they were challenged by the advantages of distance and deep penetration of the thrusting spear. In examining the human body with their mystical and patient wisdom, they determined that with patience and practice, the fingertips of the open hand could be forged to equal the thrusting, tearing power of the metal-pointed spear.

Inconceivable as it may seem to the Western mind, it *is* possible, by the use of true karate procedures, to so strengthen and condition the extended fingers, that they are able to penetrate and splinter inches of hard wood. In fact, when performed properly, your hand will be unaware of the finger-spear blow, and will have the same sensation as poking your finger into water. This is also the legendary, heart-stab, wherein the hand penetrates the opponent's solar plexus, reaching inward and upward to the heart.

Though apparently weak when untrained, determined practice can forge the hand spear into a weapon of equal power to that of a famous contemporary karate master, who, during his daily morning run, reaches down every few steps, spearing knuckle-deep into the hard-packed surface of the road, withdrawing each time with a handful of clay.

The finger-spear is a killing weapon, with the advantage of four inches of farther reach, plus concentrated penetrating power. It can be used with decisive effectiveness against the Adam's apple, sides of throat, hollow behind collar bone, solar plexus, side ribs and waist, soft point in center of lower abdomen—an especially destructive blow—kidneys, armpits, and inside of thigh.

In conditioning the finger-spear for strength and penetration, always keep the fingers slightly bent and under tension from the muscles at the base of the palm just in front of the wrist. In some hands the fingertips will form an irregular line with one finger, usually the middle one, extending farther than the ones on either side. The fingers can be evened by allowing the middle finger to to bend slightly in on contact with the mat, until it is even with the fingers on either side, before allowing it to stiffen for the blow.

As the ancient warriors who fought with bows and arrows developed both vertical and horizontal arrowheads—the first for hunting animals whose ribs ran vertically, the latter for use in the killing of men whose ribs run horizontally—so did the ancient monks, when devising the principles of the karate system for defensive use against armed men, evolve several positions of the finger-spear for more effective penetration of specific areas.

First is the palm-down spear—for deadly use against the throat, sides of neck, under nose, bottom of ribs on either side of the solar plexus, and the kidneys. Second is vertical spear for direct and shocking penetration of the solar plexus and the lower side ribs, which run vertically when your opponent is exposed by the proper karate block. Third is the palm-up spear for the heart-stab through the solar plexus, under the ribs, soft spot in center of lower abdomen, and the groin.

Practice all three for a complete, overwhelming karate arsenal.

Basic defense position: Opponent throws a right to your heart. Block with middle-chop block with your left hand, and counter immediately with left hand finger-spear to throat. (Practice with extreme caution as a strike to the Adam's apple can cause serious injury.)

Basic defense position: Opponent throws a left to your body. Block with a snapping downward and outward chop block with your left hand. Follow it immediately with a vertical right hand finger-spear to his side ribs which will be exposed by your block.

Basic defense position: Opponent throws a left hook to your head. Block it by whipping your left elbow slightly downward, across the front of your body (inside elbow block), and blocking opponent's blow with the inside of your wrist or forearm; he then follows with a right hook to your head. Sweep your left arm back across your body, maintaining the vertical angle of your forearm, blocking his blow with the inside (little finger side) of your forearm. Counter immediately with a hard penetrating palm up right hand finger-spear to solar plexus. When working this at mat, keep going for penetration—with sufficient practice you will reach the heart.

188. Snapping chop block...

189. Snaps into finger-tip spear.

190. Forearm block.

191. And snap block.

192. And palm-up poke.

Now practice these combinations in front of your mat. Do one blocking sequence, and then 10 repetitions of the poke. Work out other combinations of blocks and pokes for both hands.

A good finger-spear is a valuable weapon, but by its nature it cannot realize the full potential of its power without steady and persistent training. There are several valuable aids in bringing your fingers more rapidly into condition. Practice push-ups on the finger-tips several times a week. When you can do two sets of 15 push-ups, raise the little finger from the ground. Repeat this process until you are on only the thumb and first finger. When you can do 15 repetitions in this position, remove the thumb, and repeat this process starting with four fingers and working down to your index finger.

Another finger conditioner is to poke into loose sand. This can be in a box or a bucket. When you can poke in to your third knuckle, you may begin poking into smooth small stones.

Whether poking the mat or into the loose sand, poke as hard as you can, but, at first, from a very short distance, as little as three or four inches. Only move it further when you feel you have used your full power from the current distance. Work for increased power and penetration in your poke, remembering, as in the punch and chop, to whip your hand back immediately—the instant the blow has touched solid resistance.

Diligent practice will soon reward you with a surprise and hidden weapon of decisive capability. You will have learned and mastered a truly marvelous expression of the ancient Asian empty-handed fighting system—karate.

193. Horse at post.

194. Circle block.

195. Palm-down poke.

13
BREATHING, KIAI,*
AND THE KARATE YELL

If there is such a thing as a "secret" to karate power—the difference between a hard hit and a karate hit which can stop a man
wherever it lands—it lies in the proper use of the breath. Breathing
is a basic element of karate training and practice. All karate movement centers around the breath and the focus of the breath is the
lower abdomen. There are many theories as to why proper breathing
produces so-called "superpower," but it is better practiced than
talked about and more good for the student will come from thirty
minutes of breathing exercise than from hours of speculation.

In karate the breath is pushed into the lower abdomen between
the navel and pelvic bone: Standing in the ready position, draw a
deep breath *in through the nose* from as low a point in the trunk
as is possible; as the breath is drawn in the lower abdomen should
rise, filling with air. There should be almost *no movement of the*

---

* The momentary focusing of all the body's powers at the instant of blocking
or striking. This is accomplished through the medium of karate breathing and
the vehicle of the karate yell.

chest. The chest is only a corridor through which the air is drawn into the lower stomach.

When this has been completed, breathe *out through the mouth* at the same time *pushing down* with the upper stomach muscles so that the lower abdomen remains hard and rounded and some *air is always retained below the navel.*

Repeat this in sets of five. Then as you progress and can take the air in lower and lower and can hold in more and more on the out-breath, increase this to sets of ten and thirty. Or, as an early-morning exercise, even sets of three hundred if you can achieve the concentration. You will find that gradually the muscles of the lower abdomen, thighs, and calves will become much harder and stronger. You will also discover that your karate movements will become lighter and more efficient; your strikes will be hard and precise, and your ability to perceive and block an attack will magnify. The control of your increased power will be at your fingertips. Many students have reported that karate breathing has eliminated all feelings of fear and nervousness before an encounter, even eliminating the need of encounter by the aura of confidence and unmoving strength that is given off.

To exercise the proper function, karate breathing must be integrated with all other karate movements. An absolute, primary rule is never make an aggressive movement while breathing in. All blocks and strikes must be made on the out-breath, with the in-breath taken in between. It is not necessary to either empty or fill the lower abdomen completely on each movement; the amount of air inhaled or expelled will be determined by the specific situation. For example, in practicing the fist punch at the post take in as long a breath as possible, before going into the imaginary block. Then strike the post five times, expelling a little of the air with each hit. With practice this can be increased to the point where one in-breath will give you sufficient air for ten or more strikes. On the other hand, should the lower abdomen be more or less empty in a situation where one must go into an immediate attack, a short in-breath will be sufficient before beginning the attacking movement. This is known as the shallow in- or out-breath as opposed to the deep in- or out-breath mentioned above, but in all instances the breathing referred to occurs below the diaphragm. Karate breathing should accompany all practice.

As an expression of the breath the karate yell forms an element of every attack. Legend has it that charging tigers have been blasted to a halt by a full, complete karate scream. In more recent experience a karate yell used by experienced students has frozen an attacker in mid-punch leaving him exposed for one vital second to direct attack. The yell should accompany every block, power movement, and all conditioning practice. It is part of every out-breath. It should consist of the Oriental syllable, HUH. When this sound is formed, the muscles of the throat and chest will naturally assume proper position to help keep air in the lower abdomen. Sometimes it is desirable to make the sound silently or very low. At other times it should be loud and sharp and on some occasions the full "EarrraH-HUH" or full karate roar will be of advantage. In all cases the yell should be performed mentally even if it is not sounded. Work-out partners should practice this against each other when sparring as there is an old animal reflex which causes a person to freeze momentarily at a sudden loud noise and the karate fighter must dull this reflex by repeated exposure. In brief summation then, a karate sequence would be composed of the following coordinated procedures. Ready and set, eyes open and unblinking, aware of opponent's entire body. In and out even karate breathing, some air in lower abdomen. Body relaxed, unified, flexible. Feet strongly in contact with ground. Attack is launched. Back step. Arm block with short out-breath and low HUH. Immediate counter with forward step; long out-breath and loud HUH at instant of contact; immediate withdrawal of attacking hand. Long or short in-breath, and set for next movement.

This is karate fighting magic in action and can be accomplished by anyone through a reasonable amount of diligent, correct, and honest practice.

196. Sparring for opening.

14

THE HARD HAND: BREAK
WOOD, BRICKS, AND BULLIES

Although the spectacular part of modern karate—the shattering of
wood, brick, and tile with the naked hand or foot—is neither em-
phasized nor particularly encouraged in Power Karate, a certain
amount of experience at the actual breaking of a solid object is
regarded as a necessary skill of the well-trained karate fighter. We
recommend about thirty minutes a week after the first month or so
of training.

Breaking wood well requires a slightly different hit than post
practice because of the way it gives or moves slightly when held by
a work-out partner. This makes the strike identical with the kind
that is needed in actual combat. Also, in order to break the wood
successfully one must achieve a very heightened focus of breath,
body, and spirit. This practice is for the development of these essential and fundamental skills, rather than to emphasize how much
wood can be broken.

For chop, punch, fist-hammer, poke, and elbow start with wood
that is dry, not more than one-fourth inch thick, four inches wide,

197. Wrist block stops kick. Right ready to counter.

and short enough so that there is not too much spring when the piece is struck. When you can break a piece of this size easily, add one more piece of the same size. When you can break three or four boards this way, go back to one piece of wood, but increase the thickness by one-fourth inch. For ball-of-foot and side kick the serious student can easily start with one-half inch wood after one month or so of conditioning.

When you can break two inches of wood (one to two years training) start on bricks. Begin with lightest cinder-block available, and work up as with wood, to regular red construction brick.

Remember, out-breath at instant of hard contact in conjunction with instant withdrawal of weapon at instant of hard contact will break wood. Do not forget karate yell. If all movements are properly coordinated the hand will feel nothing as it breaks the wood. It will be like passing your hand in and out of water. If the break is clean and the bottom plank in the pile splits first the training is proceeding properly. This is why karate blows do so much damage. The damage is internal, injuring from the inside out. Remember, focus, form, and speed are the essential parts of the karate strike. Do not try to power through the wood as this will have the effect of seriously limiting your power. Do not be afraid, do not tighten up; just let go and trust in training and spirit to accomplish the job.

It is not necessary to have a heavily calloused or deformed hand to qualify as a karate fighter. Following to the letter training instructions in the manual, the student will increase tendon and bone strength, and condition the skin of the hand to where he can break wood and brick without fear of injury. The hand will show no apparent signs of karate training. The mat will provide proper conditioning for the striking points and the actual wood-breaking helps complete the process. Be patient, it is not possible to hurry the hands and feet into condition; at the same time be tenacious, as a certain amount of grit is needed in any fighting art.

198. Into diagonal stance from kick. Two blocks stop two attacks.

199. Punches over retreating arm to win.

200. Vertical elbow against two-by-four.

201. Finger-tip spear snaps inch-thick slab.

202. Form and concentration crack heavy wood with kick.

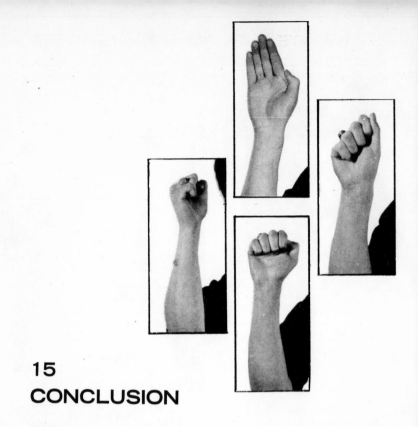

15
CONCLUSION

Power Karate is not quite a perfect system, as no system of fighting is ever perfect, but over thousands of years all the best possible movements have been evolved, and all the bad movements eliminated. Power Karate, therefore, gets as near perfection as any human endeavor is able to. How fast your own ability approaches this perfection depends on the time and intensity with which you train, and by following the system and training methods taught in this manual you can rest assured that the most productive results will be returned for your time and effort.

Remember, never underestimate anyone. Just as you are skilled at karate, so may another have acquired equal skill. Whether it is fighting, talking, or running, everyone can be good at something.

Good luck in your karate training. We trust that you will never have to employ your knowledge violently. In that case you will have reaped a full reward in health, strength, confidence, and poise from your workouts. This mental and physical growth will further success in other fields of life. Should it become necessary to demonstrate your training, your karate fighting skill will prove a sturdy friend in any emergency.